Tall Ship Sailing For Landlubbers

by

Bailey Cavender

Dedicated to my sailing family and to my parents.

To Mom, who supported me in this crazy adventure,

And to Dad, who is a sailing enthusiast and introduced

me to the wonderful world of sailing.

TABLE OF CONTENTS

Introduction: How Did I Get Here?......................1

Landlubber………………………………………....…5

Don't Knock the Pin-rail Game……………....………..12

Living With Your Co-Workers……………………..19

Education is Key…………………………………….…..25

I Didn't Know These Muscles Could Hurt…………...…32

Sailing in Film…………………………………….…35

Maintenance is King……………………………….…37

Bilge Gnome, Rig Sloth……………………………….43

Open Ocean, Tiny Human………………………….....49

Standing on Monsters……………………………....…58

Don't Forget to Sea-Stow…………………………….63

Standing Watch……………………………….……69

Minimalist, *or* My Little Cubby…………………….74

Shoreheads and Hygiene……………………………...78

Facing Fears………………………………….………83

Calm Waters, Stormy Weather……………………….94

Tours Can Be Hard...98

Epilogue: The Sea is in Your Blood...............……......102

Photo Credits..................................…………....…106

Introduction: How Did I Get Here?

Once upon a time, in a place far from the ocean and as flat as a pancake, a fresh-faced young historian was looking for a job that was a little closer to home. Wanting to try something new, she did a Google-search for "maritime history museums pacific northwest," and sent out many applications. One of those applications was to an organization that specialized in education and happened to be on a tall ship. The rest is history.

Tall ships are the stuff of dreams. Traveling using the power of the wind in their sails, they are beautifully crafted. Many tall ships are used today for educational purposes, sailing around and teaching young people about science, history, and sailing. These organizations are run by people who are dedicated to their work, who believe in the importance of these lessons, and who love the ocean and their ships. A tall ship that offers training for sailors and an educational program for students is one way that many sailors can get sucked in. In fact, this is where a young, idealistic educator and historian who liked boats on lakes enters the picture.

Look at how excited I am!

I don't want to go into too much detail here, but I will say this, loudly for the people in the back: A boat on a lake, even a sailboat, is different than a tall ship on the ocean. One more time: tall ships are a unique beast, with a strange set of wonderful, magical, and annoying quirks. You can read about them and use little boats, but there is nothing like a tall ship. That is my unbiased opinion, and I am sticking to it.

My journey into sailing was a strange one. I was not born and raised on the ocean; I'm from Idaho. I knew that I loved the ocean, and that I enjoyed being on and working with smaller boats, but I had never been on a tall ship before. I had seen pictures and read everything that I could about them. When I got on the plane to start my sailing adventure as a professional educator, I knew it would change my life. I just didn't know how much it would change my life.

Ironically, no matter what I try to do with my life, I always end up back in education in some way. I went into history specifically **not** wanting to teach, and now I find myself a high school teacher. My work on tall ships is similar. I had education experience and a love for small boats; they needed an educator who liked boats. True, I had no tall ship experience, but I'm a quick study. The only thing I hadn't counted on was my terrible fear of heights (but that's another essay entirely).

Looking back, a book on sailing for landlubbers would have been very helpful for me. This book is a combination of helpful hints to remember when sailing on a tall ship and some of my reflections on that seven-month long contract, one of the most challenging, and most rewarding, times of my entire life thus far.

Sailing changes you. You learn that you are capable of more than you ever thought possible, and there is a sense of pride in a hard day's work done well. Whether sailing, giving tours, or working on maintenance when the boats are out of water (called a haul-out), there is nothing like being on a tall ship.

Again, that is my unbiased opinion.

Landlubber

When you are a landlubber, like I was, it is important to know what you need on a tall ship. Really, you don't need to bring much. Toiletries, a nicer outfit, clothes for after stand-down, sturdy boots that have a good tread, a sleeping bag, foul weather gear, a variety of hats, a warm coat, pajamas, ibuprofen, shoes that are easy to put on quickly, a flashlight, a rig knife, and clothes that you don't mind getting dirty are all things that you should bring with you.

Why bring clothes that you don't mind getting dirty, you may ask? Well, that is because boat maintenance is an important part of sailing and it can be messy. Wearing clothes that need to be kept clean is a bit of a hassle. This is also why it's crucial to have clothes to wear after stand-down. This is the part of the day when work is completed, and everyone can relax. If you have spent the entire day sanding, varnishing, cleaning bilges, or some other form of maintenance, then you do not want to keep wearing those clothes. No, you want to take a shower, if possible, or at the very least, change your clothes and wash your face.

Despite the face I'm making, this was a lot of fun.

Personally, I dropped the ball on the whole rig knife thing. It was a misunderstanding with the person I was replacing, so I ended up not getting my rig knife until later during my adventures, but it is an important tool to have with you. One of the best parts about my rig knife is that it's a pocket rig that comes with a marlin spike at the other end. Personally, I love using the marlin spike. It's good for untying knots **and** for self-defense.

Okay, I don't know the latter for sure, but I assume it would be an effective weapon. The important thing to remember about a rig knife is to make sure it is attached to you. I used a carabiner and a rope. This way, if I dropped it while up aloft (in the rig, or, up among the sails), it wouldn't be lost to the sea or potentially hurt someone. Those things are sharp!

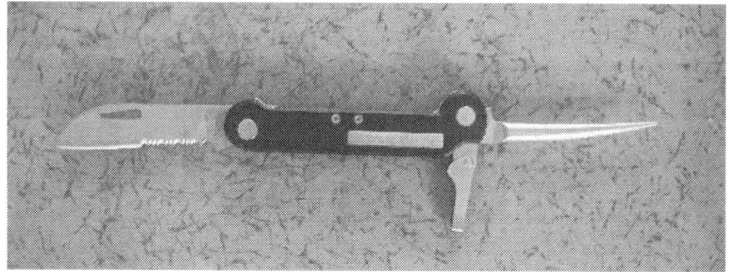
See what I mean?

I learned interesting things about myself while working on a tall ship. On the days that I am working, I will throw myself wholeheartedly into whatever task I am working on. I will climb into bilges and power sand the hull. But when I have my day off, I like to look nice.

When I left the boat on my day off, I usually left my hair down and put on earrings. Long and dangly ones. Another way that I did this was to bring a couple of scarves with me. These were easy to pack but could make me feel a little nicer. When it comes to a frivolous object, these were light and didn't take up much room.

Foulies, or foul weather gear, are a thing that you must have. These things, either pants or coveralls and a coat, keep you dry when the weather is foul., hence the name. They are made to withstand more water than typical raincoats. I got the shells, or the water-resistant part, because they were smaller to pack. To prevent condensation buildup on my clothes, I wore these shells over sweatpants and a fleece jacket. Personally, I thought that they worked very well.

Along with foulies, having the proper gear for your feet is important. If your boots do not have a good tread, you can fall and hurt yourself on the deck and on the docks.

Being able to work in conditions that are a little slick is crucial to being a safe sailor.

Safety is very important on tall ships. Not only are they equipped with engines, radios, and GPS, ships are regularly inspected by the Coast Guard. Tall ships also take the safety of their sailors very seriously. Sailing can be dangerous work. First, tie your hair back and don't wear rings. Both can get caught in lines (ropes that are doing a job) or on other parts of a ship. I was also told not to step in a coil of lines or wrap a line around my arm, because it might tighten suddenly. That would be bad. And painful.

When you are going to work aloof, you announce that you are doing so by saying, "Laying aloof" and adding whichever mast you are climbing. Then, you wait until you are given the go-ahead by your captain, who will say, "Lay away." When you get back to the deck, you have to say that you are back on deck.

If the ship is traveling from port to port, on what is called transit or being underway, there are other rules. Anytime you go on deck or leave deck, you need to announce that. This way, the people on watch know that everyone is safe.

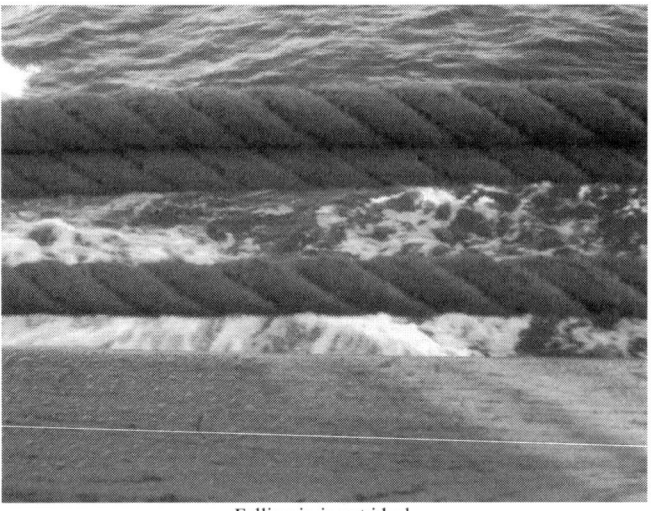
Falling in is not ideal.

If you don't announce that you are on deck and you fall overboard, no one knows to look for you. By announcing it, you are keeping yourself safe. The captain and first mate will also sometimes call out "All hands," to which everyone is excepted to respond, "All hands aye." This lets them know that the rest of the crew is listening, so that they can give the next set of instructions. Call and response is an important way that sailors keep in contact with each other and keep each other safe.

Different ships have different rules and guidelines, but these are a good reminder of what you will need, as well as some important safety rules that can be used generally on a variety of sailing vessels. Each boat will have some unique safety rules, however, since each tall ship is different than the others.

Don't Knock the Pin-rail Game

One thing to remember when you first step foot on a tall ship is that there is a lot to remember. You will get a Waistcoat Manual that will include a lot of helpful hints about the adventure that you are about to embark on. Love this manual. Don't just leaf through it one time. Read it and learn from it.

There are two pages in my waistcoat manual that I personally read over and over again before I even stepped foot on the ship I would be sailing on. These pages were the sail plan and the pin-rail diagram.

You may be asking yourself a very logical pair of questions right now. What are sail plans and pin-rail diagrams? A sail plan is just a picture of the ship with all the sails set, and each sail labeled. This is a very helpful tool.

Here is the sail plan from my Waistcoat Manual:

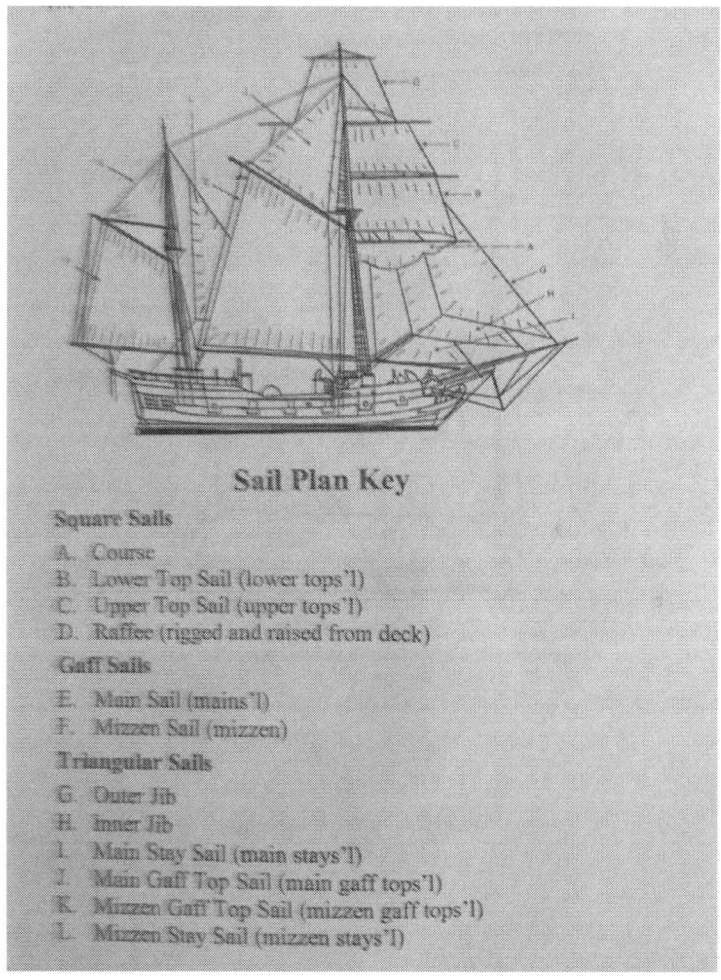

Sail Plan Key

Square Sails
A. Course
B. Lower Top Sail (lower tops'l)
C. Upper Top Sail (upper tops'l)
D. Raffee (rigged and raised from deck)

Gaff Sails
E. Main Sail (mains'l)
F. Mizzen Sail (mizzen)

Triangular Sails
G. Outer Jib
H. Inner Jib
I. Main Stay Sail (main stays'l)
J. Main Gaff Top Sail (main gaff tops'l)
K. Mizzen Gaff Top Sail (mizzen gaff tops'l)
L. Mizzen Stay Sail (mizzen stays'l)

See how everything is laid out and clearly labeled? This plan helped me become more familiar with the rig, or everything above the deck, before I even set foot on board.

It's also a handy tool to pull out when people ask me about the ship I sailed on.

The other page I clung to with a sort of desperation was even more important. This page was the Pin-rail Diagram, or the Line Location page. Each sail on the sail plan is controlled by a variety of lines, or ropes doing a job. Each line has a specific place that it goes. When setting or putting away (called dousing) sails, it is critical to know which line goes to what sail or piece of the boat.

Some lines control the boom or the yards (the wooden pieces that the sails go on). Some lines can be dangerous if they are taken off the pin-rail too early. Sometimes, other sailors can be on those yards, and if they are going to be moved, they need to get a heads-up. Since tall ships care about safety, this is all important information to know.

Here is the picture of all the lines from my Waistcoat Manual:

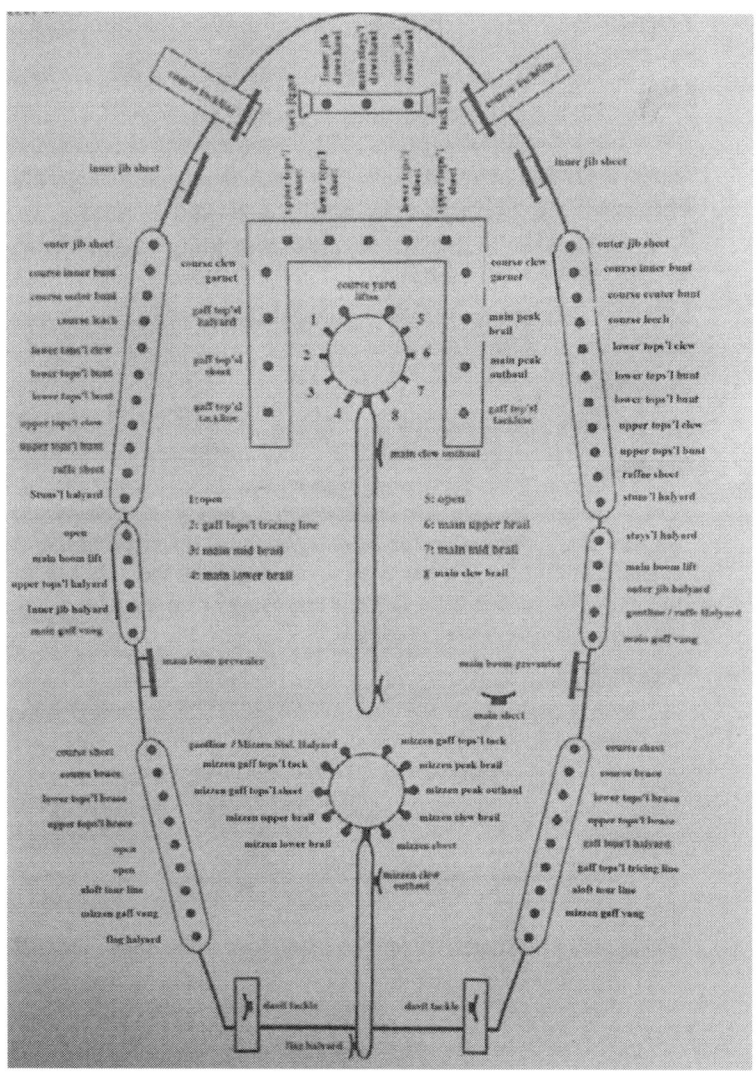

This was one of those times when having a photographic memory would have been very helpful. If you do not have one, I would recommend studying this thing. However, be aware that, when you step foot on the ship, you might find yourself a little distracted. There is so much to look at that no matter how much you studied, that will fly to the back of your brain. Or at least, it did for me and I studied that thing and the pin-rails almost every night until I had it down.

To be fair, how is this not an amazing sight?

For years, sailors did not have a diagram with all the lines and other pieces laid out so clearly for them. No, they had to learn on their feet as they were going.

That concept stresses me out even more than trying to memorize that chart. However, early sailors had a trick that modern sailors also utilize. This trick is called the Pin-rail Game.

I can hear you now. The Pin-rail Game? That sounds dumb. I can see where you would get that idea, but I will tell you that you are wrong. The Pin-rail Game is a wonderful way to make sure that your hours of studying can be applied to the actual ship, not just a picture.

Here's how it works. Someone higher up in the boat hierarchy calls one of the lines on the pin-rail. Port upper tops'l bunt, outer job sheet, mizzen gaff tops'l sheet…all of the lines are fair game. When you hear the line, it is your job to walk (not run. Don't run on boats. It's dangerous) to the place where that line is and touch it. You are trying to get to the correct line before anyone else does, and the person who is calling out the lines will either say yes or no when you touch a line.

This is a wonderful and hands-on way to become more familiar with the ship you are sailing on. The Pin-rail Game is fun. For me, it helped me fix the things I had seen in my book to the actual, real-life counterparts. It was also a way to show myself that I did know more than I thought I did.

If someone suggests the Pin-rail Game to you when you are a new sailor, dear landlubber, I would recommend that you play along. Even if you do know everything, it's a nice refresher course.

Living With Your Co-Workers

There is another thing that you might not be totally prepared for when you are starting out on your own sailing adventure. You will be living on the boat. Okay, you might be prepared for that. The other part of that equation, however, is that not only are you living on the boat, so are all your co-workers.

Everyone has their own bunk, or rack, with a curtain and a place to store their stuff, but that doesn't change the fact that you don't leave work at the end of the day and then come back. You stay there.

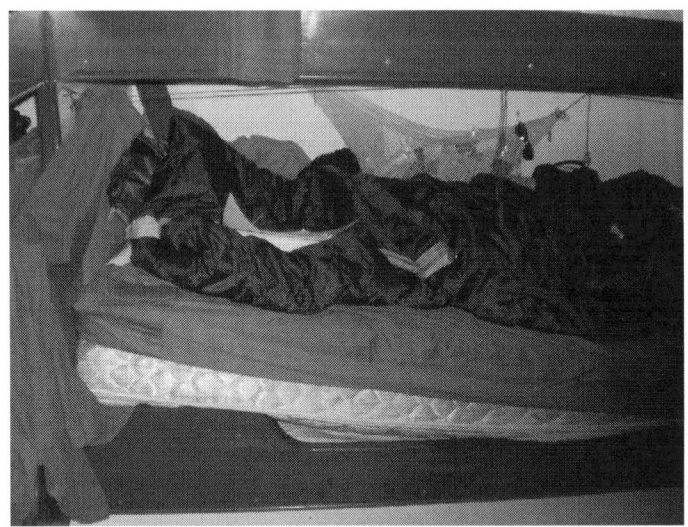
I never pretended to be tidy.

No. When work is done, you finish any chores that you must do, like taking out the trash or doing the dishes, and then you can find a place on the boat to watch television or a movie with the rest of the crew. There is only one place that you can go to be truly alone, and that is your bunk. Sure, if you are sitting quietly on deck with a book, the crew is not likely to talk to you, other than a "hi" or a smile.

There is a whole new dynamic that you need to learn when sailing. You resolve conflicts and misunderstandings in new ways. There isn't time for petty arguments or disagreements about someone putting their mug on your hanger.

But don't put your mug on someone else's hanger.

I think there are a couple of reasons for this. First, sailors are too tired to be anything but what they are. Sailors will tell you to your face when they are feeling cranky or annoyed, and then they will move on. Sailors can be blunt, but it's one of the things that I like most about them. They will be cheerful for the guests, but when it comes to the crew, it is too exhausting to wear a mask of peppiness all the time. This means that you see each other at your best and worst, and it makes the relationship among the crew that much stronger.

Secondly, sailing can be dangerous. You need to be able to trust that the people you are sailing with are going to have your best interests at heart. If you are sick, you need to trust that your crew will take care of you. If, heaven forbid, you lose your footing while climbing aloof, you need to know that your crew will do everything that they can to help you stay safe.

The biggest thing to remember is that sometimes everyone needs time for themselves. Respect that when your shipmates need it and realize when you need to take it yourself. If there is a night when you just want to take your book (or your pin-rail diagram) up to the deck and sit in silence, listening to the sounds on the docks, that's normal.

And the view is usually amazing.

Some days, it's a lot of fun to be on galley duty, or kitchen duty. I would find an audiobook or a cd and clean the galley until it was shiny and clean. Some people hated it, but I always enjoyed it. It made me take time for myself, while still keeping me connected to the crew on occasion. The galley can be a pretty popular place, you know. Especially when you're listening to the "Game of Thrones" audiobook.

Living with your coworkers is a double-edged sword. On one hand, it brings you even closer together. It is also important to remember is that you all will, occasionally, need to take some time for yourselves.

Don't be afraid to take alone time. When you have a day off, get off the boat. Go to a coffee shop and journal, visit a museum, explore the downtown, or find a park and read in the sun. Walk to the Golden Gate Bridge and take some terrible photos of yourself.

See? Awful picture, Golden Gate Bridge.

You can love your boat and your coworkers, and still take advantage of time apart, especially if you are an introverted person. Giving everyone time to decompress after a hard day's work is a critical part of crew mental health.

Education is Key

Depending on the ship that you are sailing on, you will have to do a lot with education. This might be in the form of tours, dockside educational programs, or outreach to people who interested in learning about sailing. This could also be in the form of three-hour education sails or education sails that last for a couple of days, where students learn about sailing, history, science, and navigation.

Best floating museum ever.

In a lot of ways, tall ships are like a very awesome floating museum that also functions as a sailing vessel. The fact that many tall ships have an educational focus is, in my opinion, a wonderful tool to help kids get excited about learning. They also help adults get excited about history, so that's cool too.

There is so much to learn here!

Not only are these kids getting to experience time on a tall ship, they are also learning. It's sneaky learning, which is one of the best kinds, especially when it comes to museums and nonprofit outreach.

My background is in education, so this was my specific job. Personally, I had a lot of fun organizing the programs on my ship, especially because there were some kids who had never been on the ocean before, despite living on the coast. I wanted to make sure that they had a wonderful educational experience, one that they would not forget.

If you are not in charge of education programs, you will likely still have an opportunity to teach a lesson and to work with the students. There will be a training meeting where you are told what you're expected to do.

It is fun though, because each sailor has a unique way to teach the lessons. Even though the major lesson is the same, the details vary. This makes it more fun, because everyone can let their own experiences show. As long as they remember that they are talking to students who are much younger than themselves.

Something that is important to remember when it comes time to have an educational event on a sail is that these ships are awesome. Never forget that you have the coolest job ever, and that other people are just taking everything in. Kids are going to be fascinated, so let them bask in the wonder that is your boat.

Look at how awesome this is!

When it comes time to share the important safety information, this is an important thing to remember. Wait until everyone has a chance to be amazed. If the ship is moving away from the dock, the passengers need to know the ways to stay safe and the calls and responses that they need to respond to. One important thing that they need to know is related to docking.

Docking is the process where the ship is brought back to the dock and involves tossing heavy and thick ropes called mooring lines. These mooring lines hold the ship to the dock and are therefore very important. This process needs to be quiet, and involves a thing called a fender. Fenders are big balloon-like things that help protect the sides of ships and docks. This is a fender:

It's so adorable.

With that in mind, passengers need to be aware that, while docking, they need to stay on the opposite side of the ship and not make too much noise. This allows the crew to focus on the issue at hand, docking.

There are differences that you will encounter with different age groups while working on education programs. Students who are in elementary school are typically going to be more obviously excited. They will all be excited to learn and ask a ton of questions. If you do dorky things like teach them sea shanties, which I always did, they will sing along.

When high school and middle school students come on board, however, they usually are really trying to be cool. Most of them are secretly very excited and interested, but they don't want anyone else to know. For these students, just give them time. Eventually, they'll admit that they're having fun.

The way I handled the sea shanty thing was this. If a group refused to sing because they were too cool, I just sang as loudly and off-key as possible, telling them that no one was going to look as lame as me and that the only way to not hear me was to drown me out by singing. This always worked.

Educational events might be less fun to you than things like going on a transit or doing training sails, but they are important. Not only does it help support your ship financially, it also offers a chance for kids to learn in a nonconventional way. Things like history and science come alive on tall ships in a way that they might not in a classroom setting. The other thing is that you get to introduce a whole bunch of kids to the wonder that is sailing, and that is worth taking the time.

I Didn't Know Those Muscles Could Hurt

Did you know that your shoulder muscles could hurt? Me either. When you are sailing, however, you will find that yes, they can. No matter what kind of sailing vessel you find yourself on, one thing that I can recommend without any hesitation is to bring some back and body pain relief medication. There are going to be muscles that you didn't even know you had that will be sore. For the first week or so, this will be miserable.

You will hurt all over, not because you're doing anything wrong, just because sailing uses a new set of muscles that we landlubbers do not use typically. Maybe that was just me. Either way, you will love your back and body pain reliever, but then your body will adjust, and you'll be fine.

After a while, this is just a regular day.

From climbing around in the rigging, pulling yourself over the futtock, setting the sails by pulling on the lines (called hauling lines), cleaning bilges, and doing a wide variety of other tasks, your arms will get stronger and the rest of your body will follow suit. You need to have strong legs to support yourself, and your core will also be stronger as well.

When you set out on your sailing adventure, then, just be prepared for that feeling. Your shoulders, lower back, arms, legs, and upper back will be sore. Eventually, those muscles will get used to it. They will get stronger and tougher, and you will be able to do things like hauling lines quicker and better.

Sailing in Film

I have always loved movies and television shows that feature sailing. *In the Heart of the Sea, Moby Dick, Master and Commander of the Far Side of the World, The Sea Wolf, Horatio Hornblower, Pirates of the Caribbean,* and so forth have always been things that I love. Books with sailing are also something that I love.

However, after I spent time sailing, I noticed that something changed. Suddenly, when I watched and read things with sailing in them, I knew enough to know when they were doing things badly.

Usually, films with sailing tend to use actual sailors in some capacity, so it's not too terrible. Sometimes, the actors spend time on a tall ship learning how they work, or at least have sailors on the ship being used.

Sometimes, it can be a little wonky, however. With that in mind, it is important to note that this is something that will be a little ruined for you. You will become more critical of sailing in film and literature. Though it is exciting when you see the pin rail game pop up in your favorite movie or book.

This critical eye isn't necessarily a bad thing. It can be fun to know the ways that things on ships actually work, and to be able to say things like, "Wait, that's not how that works!" At the same time, don't let your sailing knowledge get in the way of fun entertainment.

I mean, you can if you want to, I suppose, but if archaeologists can enjoy Indiana Jones, then sailors can enjoy movies where the sailing is less than accurate.

Maintenance in King

Something that you will need to remember when on your tall ship is that maintenance is king. Education may be an important part of what you do, and the sailing might be the most fun, but without the maintenance portion, everything else falls apart, sometimes literally.

There are things that need to be done daily, like dishes, taking out the trash, sweeping, and disinfecting. This keeps the ship in good shape and keeps the crew healthy. There are also other projects that are done daily like cleaning the deck and polishing the brass. These are all necessary to care for the vessel and keep it looking nice. Despite that, there are other maintenance projects as well.

You have to maintain this.

These maintenance projects include refreshing paint jobs, cleaning bilges (we'll talk about that in another chapter), cleaning storage space, cataloging costumes, doing laundry, removing rust from a variety of metal surfaces, polishing pieces of the pin rail, repairing sails, and polishing blocks. Blocks are the pieces of wood that the lines run through up in the rig, or in the places above the deck.

There are other projects that might be more specialized or specific. For example, if a sail is not torn, there is no need to repair it. Sometimes, the varnish needs to be removed and replaced on the yards, which are the horizontal stick things that the sails hang on. This varnishing job is not something that is done daily, however.

This is me on a yard.

Every so often, a ship gets to take part in what is called a haul-out. This involves taking the ship out of water and doing maintenance on it. It particularly involves repair-work and upkeep on the hull, or the bottom part of the ship. Since this part of the boat is usually under water, this is a great time to work down there. It's also a chance to do welding projects, which can be a challenge on the ocean.

Set up for haul-out.

This also involves a thing called down-rigging, where the yards are taken down so that they can be examined, varnished, painted, and any other issues that might crop up can be addressed. I think of haul out as a time to give some love and attention to the ship that works hard all year round. Then again, I enjoy things like dressing up in a full body suit with a respirator and power-sanding the bottom of the ship or climbing into and cleaning the bilges.

I'm dressed up and ready to go.

If you get a chance to help with a haul out, I would highly recommend it. Don't worry, there is a haul out activity for everyone. Some of the tasks involve climbing, if you like that sort of thing. Others, and these are the ones I look for, involve the work that most sailors dislike, the dirty and dusty ones that involve being in tight spaces with power tools. What can I say? I'm strange that way. There are some maintenance projects that you will like better than others, but they are all important. Maintenance, after all, is king.

Bilge Gnome, Rig Sloth

There are these things called bilges. I always described the bilges as place where the propellers go through the ship. The bilges take on water, but the trick is to make sure that the water is not coming in too quickly.

Every so often, the bilges need to be emptied of water and cleaned. You do this by using a shop vacuum, sucking the water out and properly disposing of it, and then cleaning the bilge with a rag and an environmentally-friendly cleaning product. This keeps things running smoothly and was one of my favorite maintenance chores.

There are bilges all over, though the biggest one on the ship I sailed on was in the main hold. The main hold was where most of the crew slept and was the biggest place on board. The bilges were especially fun for me because I liked them, was fairly good at them, and most people preferred to be aloft, so I always got to clean the bilges.

I had a running joke with a crew mate that we were bilge gnomes. We had decided that bilge gnomes lived in the bilges and stole socks. Like gnomes do. In particular, we were bilge gnomes because we were both small enough to fit inside a bilge, and both of us enjoyed working in there.

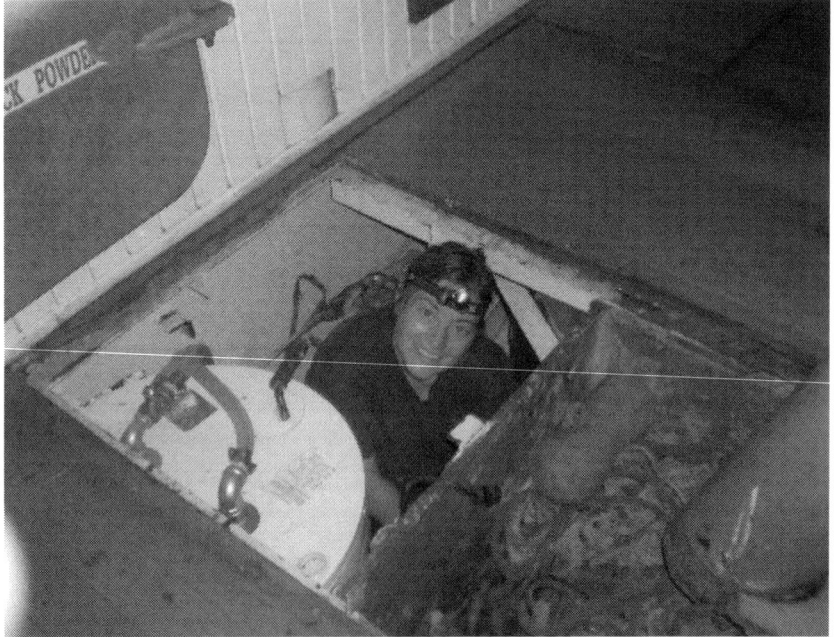

This is one of my favorite pictures of me, because I'm so excited to be in there.

If I had the option, I would have been the official bilge cleaner on the ship. Sadly, that was not a job that existed. I settled for being a bilge gnome who did not steal socks.

Most people who sail enjoy furling up aloft. Let me break that down for you a bit. Furling is when the sails are put away after they have been used. When I tell my classes about furling, I tell them that furling is the process where the sails are put away into their little sail burritos.

Tell me that you don't see the burrito analogy and I'll call you a liar.

Sailors love climbing on things. There is a wonderful view and most of them are fearless. There are places to step, sails to furl, and did I mention the awesome view? The expression "rig monkey" is an extension of this idea. Sailors tend to be very comfortable in the rig, able to move on instinct, knowing what they need to do and doing it.

There is no shortage of things to climb on.

That's a rig monkey. I was not, and never will be, a rig monkey. No. I was a rig sloth.

A rig sloth is a person who is slow up aloft. When it came time to furl or to work up in the rig, I could do it. I did do it. However, unlike other crew members, I moved very slowly and deliberately.

There I am. Deep in focus.

I'm not trying to suggest that other crew members were being unsafe. They weren't. I was just nervous and so I wanted to take my time. I got faster as time went by, but I still preferred to find a place and stay there, only moving when I had to.

In my experience, there's nothing wrong with taking your time to do your job well. As time goes by, you get faster at it. You might become a rig monkey. Maybe you will be one of the people who was always clamoring to climb up and furl.

Maybe you'll just go up when you must, because frankly, you'd rather be in the bilges. And of course, you might be a lucky sailor who enjoys both activities for various reasons. There is a place for all types.

Open Ocean, Tiny Human

One of the things that I found myself enjoying the most while sailing was this thing called a transit. A transit is, basically, the transportation of goods and peoples from place to place. This is the way that tall ships travel from place to place and is a lot of fun. Sometimes, passengers buy tickets and travel with the ships as they go from place to place, and sometimes it's just the crew.

During my seven-month contract, I was able to go on several transits, traveling from Sacramento to Oceanside, to Newport and to Aberdeen. Each of these transits taught me something new and exciting, but there was one thing that never seemed to get old. This was the idea that, really, I was kind of tiny and insignificant in the grand scheme of things.

My first transit, I took some longhand notes in my journal. Later, I transcribed this journal entry into my blog. When I was thinking about the idea of "tiny human, open ocean," I kept coming back to this idea that there is nothing like being on the open ocean to make you realize how truly tiny you are, while also realizing just how big the world around you is. Since there is nothing like those first-hand notes to explain what was going through my head, I thought I would share some things from that entry, particularly the picture I had drawn. The first thing that I wrote down was about the variety of things that I am seeing, while sitting on the deck in the sun:

"We've been on the ocean for a day or so now. I've been on watch at the magic time of 4am to 8am. Starts at night, the sun rises and suddenly it's day. I've been on the 12am to 4am slot. Less magic, but still beautiful. I was furling on the yards as we sailed under the Golden Gate Bridge (GGB). I saw two different pods of porpoises from deck. I'm long-handing this, listening to chatter of my crewmates and basking in the sun. Slightly rolling seas, temps in the high-50s to mid-60s. Glorious."

I later learned that a transit did not always mean a calm sea and beautiful weather. Sometimes, they are quick. Sometimes, there are storms, rain, and fog. And sometimes, you do, in fact, throw up because of those things. But, this time,

"I haven't thrown-up yet, but there have been a few close calls. The most memorable one was while furling in the Bay, getting ready to go under the GGB on the lower course. Got my foot stuck in the sail because it was blowing towards my footrope. I was lashing the clue-the end of the sail which must be tied up to the end of the yard- and I got my foot stuck. Then I stepped out onto the horse-little loop for feet at the end of the yard-and nearly threw-up onto the deck."

There were a lot of moments on transit where I got nervous. One of those was the time above, when I got stuck. I also learned something valuable. I learned about my ship while on a river, not an ocean. Like there is a difference between little boats and big boats, there is a difference between sailing on rivers and oceans. For one thing, a river is a little more contained. Boats don't move as much on rivers. The thing that happened in that excerpt happened in the San Francisco Bay, which was scary. The ship kept rocking and moving a lot more than I was used to. Of course, I did it (because it was my job). However, if I thought climbing aloof in the Bay was scary, I was not prepared for the open ocean. For an idea of my thoughts about what that is like, here is a sketch that I made of the first time I climbed aloof on the open ocean.

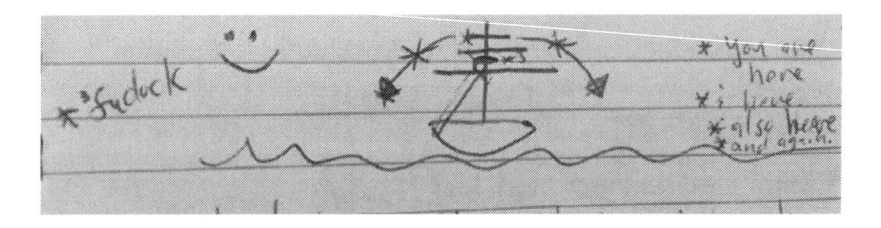

This picture might be a *slight* exaggeration, but that was the way that I felt on that first climb. Then I learned that I could really do anything. If I had a job to do, even if it involved climbing, I could do it. I also was thrilled to see that the view from up aloft was one of the most beautiful things I had ever seen in my life. So, once I got my footing, it was all worth it. From up there, you can see for miles and miles.

One of my friends has a sticker that says, "The Sea Hates You," and I love this. To me, this means that the ocean doesn't care about me or my feelings. It is huge, full of life, and has a resounding rhythm to it. But if I am sad, the ocean is not going to stop doing its thing. The ocean does not stop because I want it to. The storms don't go away because I am sad that the sun is hiding.

Really, the idea that the sea hates me isn't right. It's more that the sea is ambivalent to my existence. It doesn't care about me enough to hate me. Because of that, there is a sense of accomplishment to being able to float on a tiny little ship that is floating along on a giant surface that could, with a simple wave, take you out without batting an eye.

Look, the ocean is vast!

There is a little more about my faith in this one than in other entries, so I just wanted to give you a heads-up about that. This whole experience changed me in a lot of ways, and one of those ways was my faith. When I thought about how big the ocean was, I also considered the fact that my God is even bigger than the ocean. I had heard that saying before, but I had never really had a framework to measure that by. When I saw the ocean, and realized how truly huge it was, I thought this:

"And then I think about how grateful I am for God and His unfailing love and mercy and grace. I mean, the ocean could swat me like a gnat. God made the ocean. God calmed the ocean in rocking swells. God flooded the world. If He tells the sea to dry up, it will. I sometimes forget when I'm talking to God just how huge He is. That I'm talking with GOD. All mighty. All powerful. All loving.

It's nice to remember the all-powerful and all-mighty, because that makes amazing grace even more amazing. Because if He wanted to, He could replace us. I'm only significant because I am letting God work through me and in my life. God chose to offer grace to someone who otherwise might not have known she was lost. And that's why it's grace. Undeserved. Desperately needed. A gift from God, who in the words of song can calm a storm with His hand."

For me, the two ideas of a huge ocean and a huge God go hand in hand. The open ocean is huge. It does not care about me or my happiness. There is nothing that I can do to beat the ocean in single combat. All I can do is sail on her, respectfully and as safely as I can. But there is another piece to this puzzle. The ocean is huge, beautiful, and heartless, but the God I serve is even bigger than the ocean. He can calm an ocean storm with a wave of His hand, and that is comforting to me.

"And that is why people still sail. It's an amazing experience. Nothing like the ocean to remind you how small you are. How insignificant."

But so beautiful!

While the ocean reminds me how small and insignificant I am, it also shows me that wonder and beauty of the natural world. I may not be a significant part of the world, of course, I still have a responsibility to care for the natural world around me. However, there is a large and complex system that exists, regardless of me. When I die, the ocean will endure. The dolphins will still be swimming, ships will still be sailing, and the tide will still be coming in. And I find that beautiful. When you set out on your first transit, I hope you can see the beauty in that as well.

Standing on Monsters

Something to consider before setting out on a sailing adventure is the fact that the ocean is full of life that we don't really know anything about. Personally, I think that the ocean is scary. I'm not just saying that because of storms, or because water and wind together can cause untold levels of destruction. No, there is something else about the ocean that terrifies me. Like, really scares me. This would be the things that live there.

Despite centuries of traveling on, swimming in, and fishing from the ocean, by 2000, humanity had explored only about five percent of the ocean. The ocean itself covers over sixty percent of the world and the idea that such a large part of the world is basically unknown is scary enough. The deepest part of the ocean, the Mariana Trench, is almost seven miles deep. Basically, there is a lot of space for things to be living in the ocean.

In *Moby Dick,* Herman Melville wrote something that has stuck with me since I read it. In Chapter 35, he describes standing in the rigging like this:

There you stand, a hundred feet above the silent decks, striding along the deep, as if the masts were gigantic stilts, while beneath you and your legs, as it were, swim the hugest monsters of the sea...

This is probably supposed to be a reminder of the size and gravity of the ocean. Melville might have been trying to get his reader to consider that there is so much that we don't know about the ocean and what is down there. In my brain, this quote can be summed up to mean that when you are standing in the rig on a tall ship, it's like you are walking over monsters.

Now, I could take the practical approach here and assume that Melville was talking about giant and vengeful whales, or even huge squids, but my brain goes to creatures that I consider to be true monsters.

My monster list includes prehistoric things like megalodons, plesiosaurus, mosasaur, and the liopleurodon. Megalodons were a prehistoric shark that was the largest shark to ever swim in the ocean, reaching lengths of up to sixty-five feet long. Plesiosaurus' were a long-necked marine hunter that could be up to forty feet long. Mosasaurs' had heads like crocodiles and could grow to be fifty-feet long. The liopleurodon was over twenty feet long. Their jaw alone was over eight feet long.

Now, I know that these are prehistoric creatures and thought to be extinct. However, there are other creatures that were thought to be long-extinct but then discovered. One of these creatures is the coelacanths, a prehistoric fish that everyone thought was extinct until it was discovered to be alive and well. If the coelacanth was found to be alive, what else could be hiding in the ninety-five percent of seventy-percent of the Earth's surface that we know nothing about?

There is a scene in almost every book with a giant shark or vengeful whale where the sea creature does something like swallow a ship whole, knocks over the ship with a swipe of its tale, or just charges it, thereby taking the ship out and throwing the crew into chaos. Could there really be a giant monster, swimming beneath my feet whenever I climb into the rigging? Could there be a large shark, looking up at the keel of my ship, wondering how we would taste? Is this a helpful train of thought?

No. No, it was not. In fact, once this idea entered my brain, I did everything in my power to keep these thoughts away. I tried to focus on dolphins, waves, and the sunrise, actively ignoring the fact that, when sailing, I could be standing over monsters.

While I was sailing, I avoided reading books like the *Meg* series by Steve Alten, *Jaws,* and other books about sharks attacking things. I also didn't read books like *Moby Dick.* Instead, I read books about sailing methods, sailing history, and things that had absolutely no connection to the ocean. I did not want to have my brain filled with the idea of giant prehistoric sharks that could swallow ships whole, or vengeful whales. Depending on how you feel about the ocean, this is a choice I would recommend. Choose your reading material wisely, and never forget that, when you are sailing, you are standing on monsters.

Or, you know what, never mind. Just forget that. It's a silly and scary notion. It's not like there is a ton of space in the ocean that is unexplored…oh wait.

Drat.

Think about dolphins, waves, sunsets, and how lovely the ocean smells. And read books that are not related to prehistoric creatures, shipwrecks, or giant and vengeful whales. It's just better that way.

Trust me.

Don't Forget to Sea-Stow

I'm going to be honest, this one is more of a friendly public service announcement. Sea-stowing is the practice of making sure that everything is lashed down when a ship is underway, or on the ocean. There are a couple of different components to this.

First, everything needs to be tied down. When you are out at sea, things tend to move. Boats do not just stay in one steady place. They tend to roll. This picture is my interpretation of how much a ship moves while on the ocean, and while it is an exaggeration, that doesn't change the fact that things still move.

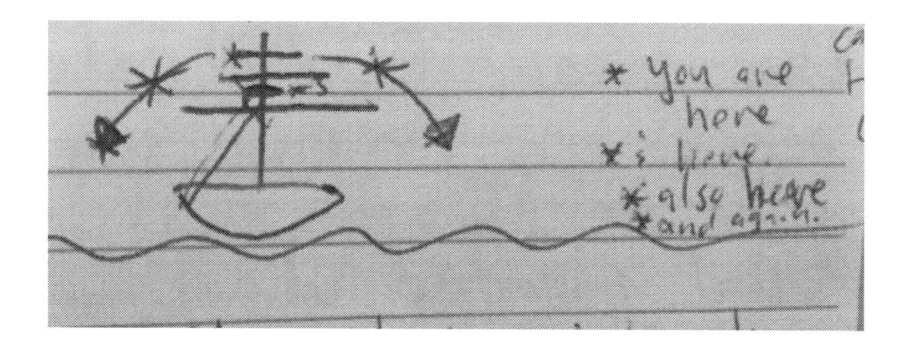

Remember this picture?

If you have stuff just laying all over the place all willy-nilly, it will move. That is why every bunk, or rack, has one of those little hammocks for your stuff. Without your stuff-hammock, things can go everywhere. No one wants to lose their stuff to the inside of the boat, or have their belongings flung all over the communal living space!

See all my stuff in its hammock?

Sea-stowing is also important to think about with the rest of the boat. The galley needs to be sea-stowed, and if you use something, you need to make sure that you return it to its proper, sea-stowed place.

The other things to remember are hatches and doors. I'm going to be honest, the door/hatch thing can be a little confusing to us landlubbers at first. The best description that I found of the differences between hatches and doors is this. Which direction are they going? If it is leading up or down, i.e., is on the floor, ceiling, or the deck, it's a hatch. If it looks like a door and goes from compartment to compartment, it's a door. For example, this is a doorway:

Pretty standard.

Anytime you open one, you need to announce that "hatch is lively," and when you close it, you say "hatch is secure." This thing that looks like it slides is a fancy hatch:

See? Fancy and sliding!

When walking around a ship, you need to be aware of any hatches. No one wants to fall into a hatch. Not only is it dangerous, it's embarrassing.

If there is a door, you need to make sure that it is either securely closed or securely opened. Hatches fit into their places, and doors have handles that need to be put all the way into place. If a door is open, it needs to be attached to the wall or space behind it.

Free-swinging and heavy doors can cause a lot of problems and seriously hurt people. On a transit, these rules are even more important. While closing doors and hatches properly is not, technically, sea-stowing, it is an important part of the process.

To me, sea-stowing is just getting the boat and the crew ready to go on the ocean for an extended period. It's tying things down, remembering your on-deck calls, and getting things ready in the galley. It also involves making sure that the deck guns are secure and won't slide all over the deck.

Deck guns are fun.

See? You do not want that to be moving all over the place. If you sea-stow badly, it means that when you get to port, you get to clean everything up. Hooray.

Yup. Sea-stowing is all about tying things down, so they don't fly all over the place.

Standing Watch

When you are on a transit, traveling between ports, there is a thing called standing watch. Standing watch is a system that considers the fact that no one is at their best when they have not slept in over a day, and that ships do not sail themselves. At least three people stand watch together. One person is steering, or manning the helm, at least one other person is the lookout, and someone else is available to do boat checks. Let me back up.

These teams work in a four-hours-on, eight-hours-off, sort of way. You and your team have the bridge, as it were, for four hours. Then you rotate out and another team takes over. After sleeping for eight or so hours, the next watch wakes you up and you relieve them.

Personally, I loved standing watch. At the end of my tour, I started having problems sleeping, unless we were on a transit. The rock of the ship put me right to sleep.

When you're on watch, there are a couple of things to keep in mind. First, if you are steering, don't panic. Someone will explain it to you when you get there. Second, whenever you're on deck during a transit, you need to have your climbing harness on.

Safety rope to prevent falling. Or give you something to grab.

Sometimes, there is an emergency up among the sails that you will need to take care of, and sometimes it's just a nice day to go sailing. The safety harness has another benefit, though. If there is a serious storm or gale, you can clip your harness to the ship itself, to prevent you from moving too much or, heaven forbid, falling overboard.

    I always clipped myself into the ratlines, the side things that you climb on, when I was standing watch. The lookout's jobs are simple, but also not. They are there to keep an eye out at the ocean and to let the helmsman, who is steering, know if they see anything that the ship should avoid. Lobster pots, other boats, rocks…these are all things that the lookout is looking out for.

I can't emphasis the view enough.

Boat checks are a lot of fun. They involve checking the bilges and making sure that the ship is not taking on too much water. You do this by taking a boat check form around and timing the drops. You check the props in the main hold bilges (another reason to sea-stow. You don't want stuff falling in the bilges), and then you check the pressure in the engine room on several instruments.

When you are done, you report back to your watch leader, and if they feel concerned, they send someone to ask the engineer or the captain for further instructions. Boat checks let you make sure that the boat is running in tip-top shape and must be done at regular intervals. Your watch leader will report what has happened in your watch to the next watch leader.

Personally, I loved the 4 to 8 Watch and the 8 to 12 Watch the best. Though the 12 to 4 isn't awful either. Most people love the 4 to 8 Watch because it includes sunrises and sunsets. It's just the prettiest watch.

This, but a whole ocean of it.

But I love the 8 to 12 Watch too. This watch has the beautiful night sky, with the moon and the stars reflecting on the water. One of these is cold, because it's midnight, but the other one is when the sun has just come up. It's warm and pretty. Honestly, there are reasons to love every watch.

Minimalist, *or* My Little Cubby

Something else that you need to consider when you are setting out on your sailing adventure is the fact that you are going to be living the life of a minimalist. There is nothing wrong with that, but it does involve certain lifestyle changes. For example, I am an avid reader and I had to choose the books that I wanted to read over seven months. I ended up with five books that I reread over and over on my tour. The space that you have on board is a small one. You have a bunk and a Tupperware bin to put any overflow objects.

Here is a picture of my bunk and the little net that held my things:

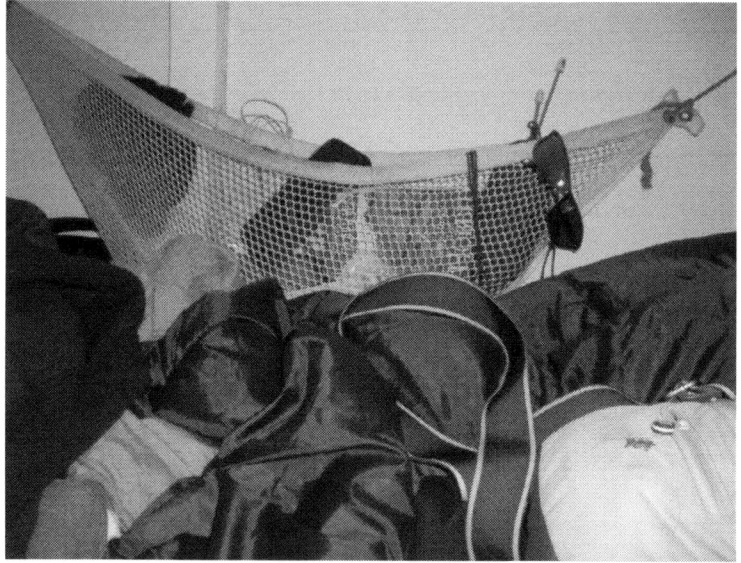

Also pictured: The Hobbit

I also visited bookstores and purchased new books that I read on my tour. Most of these books would later be donated to the boat library or to a local thrift store, because if it didn't fit in my bunk, I could not keep it. Later, I moved to the fo'c'sle, and I had one of the shelves for my books. I did enjoy that.

The story of my move to the fo'c'sle is a funny one. Basically, I was one of the officers and one of the lower-ranking ones. There was an opening in the fo'c'sle for an officer, and the officers ahead of me didn't want to move. The beds that were available, you see, where shorter than the ones in the main cabin. Since I didn't mind a short bed, being a short woman, I got to move.

This is one of the larger bunks.

If you think that you might not be okay with living a minimalist lifestyle, that is a valid concern about your future on a tall ship. As time goes by, however, you get used to it. You learn just how much you don't need.

I like having fifty books near me, but if I must choose between having a ton of books and having shampoo and clean socks, I'm going to go with socks. Some books will be present, but not fifty.

Shoreheads and Hygiene

Whenever I talk to people about my time on boats, one of the first questions that they ask is always about hygiene. So, let's address that now; you've been more than patient, dear landlubber.

Hygiene on a tall ship can be a little strange. Sure, there is a shower on board, but the water from that gets filtered into the grey, or dirty, water tank, and the water that goes into it comes from the ship's water supply. If you are at a dock, you're connected to shore water, but still. Because of this, showers are not an everyday occurrence. I showered at least once a week, usually on my day off. If I had been involved in a particularly dirty maintenance project, I would shower, but otherwise it wasn't as important.

This day, I showered.

The other consideration was that I lived with many other people, and didn't want to be a shower pig, using more than my allotted shower shares. It was also not just me. Everyone viewed showers that way, to an extent. After a while, your hair gets used to it and isn't as greasy, which is nice.

The one time that I remember the entire crew being told to go and not come back until we smelled better was after my first big transit. This was a long trip, and apparently, we all smelled bad. Our captain kicked us all off the boat with a bag of quarters and told us that we were not allowed back until we had all showered.

Sometimes, the port you're docked at will have showers. Sometimes these will be coin-operated. Someone on the boat will be in charge of finding that information out for you and the rest of the crew. Other times, there will be no shower services available for you at the port. Sometimes, local hotels will donate a room for tired sailors to have a place to go watch tv and sleep in a real bed. And there are boat friends in most ports, willing to help sailors out with rides and places to shower.

We turn our attention now to the concept of a shorehead. A head is what the restroom on the ship is called, so a shorehead is a bathroom on shore. Whenever possible, it is advised to use the shorehead. The heads on the ship fill up the black water tank, which has a limited amount of space in it.

A shorehead can be a variety of things. These can be a couple of port-a-potties, the bathroom at the marina or dock, the public restroom near the ships, or, on occasion, a local business will allow you to use their restrooms. If you are leaving to use the shorehead, make sure that you tell someone. I always took my rig knife, just in case (but in my pocket, so it didn't look like I was trying to start a fight).

For some people, this is the hardest part of being on a ship. Using public restrooms, fewer showers…it can take some getting used to. But you can still brush your teeth.

And remember, this is where you work.

Seriously.

Facing Fears

You may not have guessed this from reading the rest of this book, but there were a lot of fears that I had to face when I became a tall ship sailor. In fact, you may have noticed the fears that I faced the most. Sea creatures, storms, and heights. Of all three of these fears, however, the one that I faced the most and feel the proudest of was the heights one.

Sure, I encountered storms and rough seas, but I never met the Kraken or a megalodon. What I did have to face was my fear of heights. I hate heights. I hate heights like Indiana Jones (and I) hate snakes. To be fair, my biggest fear is falling from heights. So, cliff jumping and bungy cords do not appeal to me in the slightest.

Here's the thing though. If you want to be an effective sailor and you are afraid of heights, you must find an effective work-around. Sometimes this is just practice, sometimes it's stubbornness. For me, it was a combination of the two. I was so scared the first time I tried to go aloof. My whole body froze up and I couldn't move.

When it came to being in the head rig, or the sails in the front of the boat, I was fine. I could hang all over that thing, no problem. Loved it. This is the head rig:

This place is fun.

For me, it was the masts that were a problem. Finally, I was informed that if I wanted to stay part of the crew, I would climb. I had no choice. I couldn't be a bilge gnome or a head-rig guru. I was mad, scared, and determined. I climbed the thing. Twice.

To be completely honest, I threw up later. One of the only times that I did so. But still.

To be fair, this was probably the most effective way to get me to climb. I was so mad that I forgot to be scared. After a while, I got used to it and I did become particularly attached to the mizzen, or the mast behind the ship's wheel. I loved furling that sail and even trained some people on how to furl it later.

The mizzen mast

    The biggest hurdle I faced was this thing called the futtock. The futtock is a platform partway up the masts where you can stop and regroup. The problem with getting to the futtock, however, is that it's not a straight climb. No, that would be too easy.

Here is me, climbing the futtock in four pictures:

Climbing.

Going over the futtock.

Pulling myself up.

Victorious!

It's hard to explain in words but let me try anyway. The first picture shows me climbing. It's straightforward. Vertical ascension.

In the second picture, also taken from the deck of the ship, you can see how my back is to the deck? That's because the process for climbing the futtock is to clip in and climb up and over the futtock. It's a moment of using your legs to push yourself up and over, while using your arms to pull yourself over the platform. You get a grip on the top of the platform and then you just go. The third picture is me, pulling myself up.

Finally, the fourth picture is me, smiling triumphantly, because I did it. No matter what, I never enjoyed that moment in picture three. I was always afraid that I would not be able to pull myself up and that I would dangle there horribly for a while. But I learned that once I got up there, I was less scared. I think this was because I knew that I had a job to do. Plus, the view was amazing.

Even though I still am not a fan of heights, I know that, if I need to go somewhere with heights, I can handle it.

This leads me to another story that is slightly less pleasant. That's the time I almost fell off of the upper topsail yard. This yard is the one farthest from the water. One time, I was up there, looking for something. It doesn't matter what it was, just that I had a reason for being up there. The yards were braced, which means that the whole mast was turned in a specific direction to catch the wind better. This made sailing more fun, but it also made climbing more challenging.

This is a normal bracing situation:

Fairly standard.

Looking back, I should have gone up to the top and stepped down onto the yard, but I didn't realize that at the time. Seriously though. If you are also a person with little legs and short arms, do this.

The mast from the deck.

I clipped in and tried to get to the foot rope the usual way, thinking, like most short people, that I was taller than I actually am. While my feet reached the footrope, my arms could not reach the yard. I floundered there in panic for what seemed like ages, when a crew member came up behind me and gave me a push. Then he sat with me for a few minutes until I could breathe again and found the thing I was supposed to find.

See? Crewmates save lives!

That night, we got back to the dock and needed to furl the sails. I knew that one of those sails was the upper topsail. I did not want to go up there. I did not want to go up there ever again. But I knew that if I didn't go up there this time, I would never go again. So, that night, I went up and furled the upper topsail, and the falling fear curse was broken.

It's important to remember that there are going to be things about tall ship sailing that scare the hell out of you. Some people hate the head rig, while others cannot stand being in bilges. Find your fear, acknowledge it, and face it head-on. Then you'll be a stronger sailor. Face your fears. It's worth it.

Calm Waters, Stormy Weather

Something important to remember is that you are not always going to have smooth seas when you are sailing. Sometimes, the ocean does not cooperate with your plans. Here are some pictures taken on different days.

Some days are grey.

Some days are rainy.

And some days are clear.

Some transits, you can travel by sail almost the whole way, and other times, you have to motor. Oh, that's another thing. Tall ships have modern engines. It's important to me that you know that.

When I was in the San Francisco Bay, there was a storm at sea that funneled into the Bay. Often, we would set our sails, and sail away from the dock for an hour or three (the *Gilligan's Island* jokes never got old to me). These would be either for education programs or for an Adventure Sail, when we would have passengers on board. Then we would float around and use the sails to sail, feeling the wind in our hair and the sun on our backs.

Back to my story. That day, we had a couple of sails and they wanted to go out. So, we did. It was raining and cold, the wind was blowing, sails were coming unfurled, the dirty water tank was malfunctioning, and the passengers were throwing up. Some days are like that, even on tall ships. Some days have perfect weather, and most days are just right.

No matter the weather, remember this. You are sailing on a tall ship. You are headed somewhere to help other people see the beauty and majesty that you get to experience every day. Sure, you get to see all the unglamorous things too, but I think that makes it better. Even the stormy weather helps you appreciate the calm days even more.

Tours Can Be Hard

One thing that you might not be prepared for when it comes to leading your own sailing adventure is the tours. The ship that I was on had tours almost every night, where we would dress up in our period-appropriate clothing, station ourselves around the deck and below deck, and on the dock, and let people explore the ship. There were places that they could not go, of course, but we were always ready with a happy smile, information, and answers to any questions.

"Can I spin the wheel? What's that gold thing? What are all the ropes for?"

There were also special sails, where the public could come and sail with us. Sometimes, we would shoot blank shots from our deck guns at other ships, and sometimes we would just sail around. These were often a lot of fun. People always got excited and loved to help sail. One time, we did a themed sail, where we dressed up like Peter Pan and the Lost Boys. People loved it. I was Wendy.

I think I'm kind of adorable in this one.

I worked as the public relations person on my boat, and as a result, I was always ON. I did not feel like I could be grumpy or unhappy, since that could impact the way that the guests felt. Was this true? Probably not, but since I am naturally cheerful, this worked out well for me.

Somedays, you are not going to want to have tours or be involved in any public outreach. Some days, you have had numerous education sails and the last thing you want to do is stand there and answer questions for an hour. Everyone is tired. Remember this, though. Not everyone is living on a tall ship. Don't forget the beauty of what you are doing.

Tall ships are pretty.

Tours are important, and I'm not just saying that because it was my job. People love them, and for some people, those are the only times that they will be able to step foot on your boat. It's actually a tremendous honor to show off the awesomeness of a tall ship.

Epilogue-The Sea is in Your Blood

Most people have a reason for seeking out adventure on the ocean. Some people are drawn to the minimalist and adventurous lifestyle. The life of a sailor is full of hard work, but also involves traveling to beautiful and exciting places in one of the most rewarding ways possible. Other people grew up on the ocean and this is just a logical next step.

And then you have people like me. I grew up in Idaho, far away from the ocean. Visiting the ocean was a special treat, something that happened every so often. Despite that, the sea was in my blood.

Once you see the sea, you're in love. Too cliché?

    You see, my family is originally from Massachusetts, and there are lots of stories that I have heard from my family about time spent on the coast. My uncle even served in the Navy.

    The biggest influence in my desire to sail, however, came from my dad. My dad was a member of the Coast Guard and a sailing enthusiast when he left the service. One of my dreams is to buy my dad a sailboat someday, so that he can sail on the nearby lake whenever he wants to. With my dad sharing his own sailing stories and encouraging me to read things about sailing and the ocean, I suppose it was inevitable that I would be a fan of the ocean.

It sounds cliché to say that sailing is in my blood, but despite being raised in a mountainous forest, I was still drawn to the ocean. Most everyone in my family had a wonderful story about the ocean to share, and it makes sense that that would carry over to me.

How can you grow up hearing about the clear, deep blue waters of the Caribbean, crabbing on the beach, sharks, storms, standing watch, sailing smaller crafts, and the port of New Bedford without wondering about life on a boat? I certainly did not.

There are a few things that bring me calm and a sense of peace. Being out in a forest, surrounded by the smell of pine trees and hearing the wind whistling in the trees, being in a giant bookstore or a church, and being on or near the ocean. The smell of the water, the feel of the spray in my face, these are the things that make my soul happy.

I can't explain it.

It might not make sense, but I suppose it just proves that the sea is in my blood.

Thanks a lot, Dad.

No, really. Thanks.

All photos are taken by or of the author.

Photos used with permission from Grays Harbor Historical Seaport Authority.

Photos of the Sailing Vessel "The Hawaiian Chieftain," 2012-2018

Work Cited

Melville, Herman. *Moby Dick or The Whale*. Ed. Herchel Parker and Harrison Hayford. New York: Norton, 2002. Print.

Printed in Poland
by Amazon Fulfillment
Poland Sp. z o.o., Wrocław
25 July 2022

37f159c1-b665-4378-a0be-f9e31aaf67feR01